On

by Alan Davison

Shield Publishers
ISBN– 13: 978-0966144192
ISBN– 10: 0966144198

There are many birds and bees today, said Pablo.

Yes, said Bonny, in the spring there are often many
birds and bees.

What are you reading? said Bonny. *Walden* by Henry
David Thoreau, said Pablo. What's it about? It's about
the year Thoreau spent living in a one-room cabin on
Walden Pond. That sounds like fun, said Bonny. Yes,
said Pablo, it does. Should we do it? Do what? said
Pablo. Live in a cabin on Walden Pond. Really? said
Pablo. Sure, said Bonny. Well, said Pablo, I'd have to
get Blurtso to watch the greenhouse...

Really? said Blurtso. Yes, said Pablo,
Bonny, Ditto and I are moving to Concord.

I suppose most of the world, said Pablo,
has rushed off to the future.

The balcony was a great idea...

We should make plans for the future, said Pablo. The future? said Bonny. Yes, said Pablo, what are we going to do? We'll be together, said Bonny. Yes, said Pablo, but what will we do? We'll walk around, said Bonny. And then? said Pablo. Then we'll eat and drink, said Bonny. And then? said Pablo. Then we'll sleep. And then? said Pablo. Then we'll walk around. And then? said Pablo. Then we'll eat and drink. And then? said Pablo. Then we'll sleep. And the next day? said Pablo. Yes, said Bonny, and the next day. Wow, said Pablo, that sounds wonderful. Yes, said Bonny, it truly does.

I like to watch the light flickering on the ceiling, said Pablo, and hear the sound of a train in the distance… the last train to Boston. Just imagine all the people, staring out the windows, seeing their reflections in the glass. I wonder what they're thinking? I don't know, said Bonny, is there any more popcorn?

Over the hill and through the woods…

…to my greenhouse I will go.

I'll fill a wagon and return to our cabin…

…where we'll all live like H.D. Thoreau.

See, said Bonny, how the grass bends in the wind?

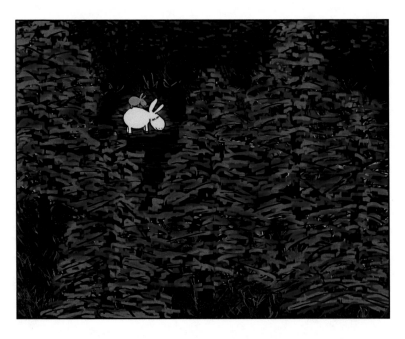

If you look closely, said Bonny,
you can see the trail of water bugs on the water.

Yes, Ditto, there are many flies today… Now, the
first step in painting a beautiful canvas is to choose
an inspirational subject—a subject that expresses the
humility and grandeur of nature…

Excellent! said Bonny.

Hmm, thought Blurtso, the cooling air makes the grass smell sweet, and the sounds more distinct—a raven, an owl, the echo of an axe—and the quickening pulse of the crickets.

Feeding the fish? said Pablo. Yes, said Blurtso, from the edge of the river, there must have been a dozen people doing it. You mean "fishing," said Pablo. Fishing? said Blurtso. Yes, said Pablo, they have a hook on the end of their line which they bait with something tasty, and they try to get the fish to bite it. The hook? said Blurtso. Yes, said Pablo, so it will push through the lip of the fish and they can pull it to shore. That's not very nice, said Blurtso. What if they did it without a hook? Without a hook? said Pablo. Yes, said Blurtso, just put some food on the line and throw it in the stream, so the fish can eat. Well, said Pablo, you wouldn't catch anything, but you might make some friends.

13

How do I know when it's done?

O.k., said Bonny, you can read the next sentence. "Sell your clothes and keep your thoughts," read Ditto, "If I were confined to a corner of a garret all my days, like a spider, the world would be just as large to me while I had my thoughts... from an army of three divisions one can take away its general, and put it in disorder, but from the man the most abject and vulgar one cannot take away his thought." Very good! said Bonny. What does "abject" mean? said Ditto. "Abject," said Bonny, refers to someone who has been reduced to hopelessness or despair. What about "vulgar"? said Ditto. In this sentence, said Bonny, it means "common" or "uncultivated." So is Thoreau saying, said Ditto, that even someone who has nothing still has his thoughts? Yes, said Bonny. And you shouldn't let anyone, said Ditto, take away your thoughts? Yes, said Bonny, as Thoreau's friend—Ralph Waldo Emerson—said, "You are what you think about all day long." That's wise, said Ditto.

16

When painting a "nature" canvas, said Bonny,
the artist must become one with the subject
in order to reveal its innermost secrets.

Excellent! said Bonny.

Where are Bonny and Ditto? said Blurtso. They're out for
Ditto's daily lesson. Bonny is always teaching him
something useful and profound.

Why aren't you painting? said Pablo. I ran out of paint, said Bonny. Oh, said Pablo, I guess you'll have to go to town.

How much for this one? said the tourist. This one? said Bonny. This one is eight tubes of paint and four canvasses. What? said the tourist. Eight tubes of paint and four canvasses, said Bonny. Don't you accept cash? said the tourist. No, said Bonny. American Express? said the tourist. No, said Bonny. Where can I get eight tubes of paint and four canvasses? In the Arts and Crafts store around the corner. O.k., said the tourist.

Today we'll focus on color, said Bonny, and explore its variety, its juxtaposition, and its infinite potential for expression…

Excellent! said Bonny

The water is certainly clear, thought Ditto. It's so clear I can't even see myself, unless those rocks at the bottom are me... Hmm... maybe those rocks at the bottom *are* me. It's nice to be a rock in the stream, on a hot day in August.

Sure, said Pablo, I see it now.

How are things at Harvard? said Harlan. They're o.k., said Blurtso, but I wish the classes were more social. Like what? said Harlan. I don't know, said Blurtso, like this. Like this? said Harlan. Yes, said Blurtso, like what we're doing now. Harvard is too rigid, and the classes are too big. It would be better if there were only five or six students, just sitting around answering questions. What kind of questions? said Harlan. Any kind, said Blurtso. How about yes or no questions? said Harlan. No, said Blurtso, that would be too limiting. How about the 5 w's and 1 h questions? said Harlan. **What**? said Blurtso. Yes, said Harlan, "what" is the first of the "w" questions. It is? said Blurtso. Yes, said Harlan, the five w's are "what, who, when, where, why,"

and the h question is "how." Why, said Blurtso, don't they call them the 6 w&h questions? That's a good question, said Harlan. See what I mean, said Blurtso, **why** can't there be a university where students just sit around talking like we are? There can, said Harlan. **How?** said Blurtso. We can start one ourselves, said Harlan. A university? said Blurtso. Sure, said Harlan. **Where?** said Blurtso. Anywhere, said Harlan, in the house or the barn, or here in the park. **Who** would teach the classes? said Blurtso. We would, said Harlan, and Bonny and Pablo could help. I like it! said Blurtso. **When** can we start? Right now, said Harlan, as soon as we get some students. Let's do it! said Blurtso.

What's that? said Blurtso. That's the logo for our university. The logo? said Blurtso. Yes, said Harlan. Weohryant? said Blurtso. Yes, said Harlan, pronounced "we-orient." What does it mean? said Blurtso. It's a word, said Harlan, made

WEOHRYANT

"We Orient U"

(letting life find itself since XXXIIIM B.C.)

up of all the different letters in the question words "what, where, who, how, when, why", and it's also a combination of we (short for "west") and ohryant (orient or "east"). And, said Blurtso, it combines U (you) and WE, which gives our university an inclusive feel. Exactly, said Harlan. What, said Blurtso, is that Roman numeral. That, said Harlan, can either be read as 967 (1000 – 33) or 33,000. Which is it? said Blurtso. It really doesn't matter, said Harlan, as long as it expresses a sense of tradition and substance. 33,000 B.C. is an approximate date for the beginning of written language on earth. I like it, said Blurtso, and the donkey looks attentive and energetic, while the elephant looks very professorial.

We had over three thousand applications to our university, said Harlan. Wow, said Blurtso, what will be the criteria for getting in? I think we should choose the first six, said Harlan. Yes, said Blurtso, "first come, first serve" is an excellent criterion, but I'm worried. Worried? said Harlan. Yes, said Blurtso, teaching is a tremendous responsibility. Yes it is, said Harlan. What if I'm not good at it? You'll be fine, said Harlan. What if my students ask questions I can't answer? Then tell them you don't know, said Harlan. Can I do that? said Blurtso. Of course, said Harlan. I thought a teacher was supposed to know all the answers. No, said Harlan, a teacher is supposed to know the questions. The questions? said Blurtso. Yes, said Harlan, the questions are more important than the answers. They are? said Blurtso. Certainly, said Harlan. Why? said Blurtso. Because many questions have many answers, and others have no answer at all. So all I have to do is ask questions? said Blurtso. Yes, said Harlan. What kind of questions? Just like the ones you're asking right now, said Harlan. The ones I'm asking right now? said Blurtso. Yes, said Harlan. I can do that, said Blurtso.

recent photo:

Name: Frank the bird
Species: Corvus Edgarallanpoeis

why did you choose Weohryant?

I live in the eaves of Blurtso's barn.

recent photo:

Name: Chelsea the donkey
Species: Asinus Femininus

why did you choose Weohryant?

I would like to purchase a hoodie with the adorable Weohryant logo!

recent photo:

Name: Glouster the Duck
Species: Quackus Platyrhynchos

why did you choose Weohryant?

The reputation of Weohryant is renowned throughout the world.

recent photo:

Name: Emma Lou Porcupine
Species: rodentia spineycomorplus

why did you choose Weohryant?

Because it is free.

recent photo:

Name: MORTON THE DONKEY
Species: ASINUS TRANQUILLIUS

why did you choose Weohryant?

WHAT IS WEOHRYANT?

recent photo:

Name:

Species:

why did you choose Weohryant?

A university? said Pablo. Yes, said Blurtso, and we need more professors. What would I teach? said Pablo. You'd teach Where-101. Is that, said Pablo, a class about gardening? It can be, said Blurtso, as long as the questions begin with "where." How many days does it meet? said Pablo. Once a week, said Blurtso. O.k., said Pablo. And what about me? said Bonny. What would you like to teach? said Blurtso. I don't know, said Bonny, maybe a reading class. Reading? said Blurtso. Yes, said Bonny, what are your students going to read? Nothing, said Blurtso, we're just going to talk. If your students read something, said Bonny, the discussions will be more interesting. You may be right, said Blurtso, what do you suggest? I think we should begin with the classic Hindu, Christian, and Muslim texts, then move to the Ancient Greek and Chinese. I'll prepare a list and get the books from the Boston Public Library. Does that mean, said Blurtso, I have to read the books as well?

Welcome, said Harlan, to the inaugural, first-year orientation at Weohryant University. It is my pleasure to introduce the faculty who will be with you for the next four years. To my left is the co-founder of the college, Mr. Blurtso Lundif. Mr. Lundif will be teaching What-101 every Monday in his barn from noon until dusk. To my right is Ms. Bonny Bray, who has prepared a reading list of Masterpieces of World Literature. She will be available on Thursdays during the day, and will serve home-made pumpkin pie that evening here in the main house. To Bonny's right is Pablo the Gardener. Mr. Gardener will be teaching When-101 on Tuesdays from sunrise until noon at the Clippety Clop Animal Refuge and Co-Op. And I, said Harlan, am Mr. Harlan de Borneo. I will be leading the discussions in Where-101 every Wednesday on the Boston Common from sometime after breakfast until sometime before lunch.

The texts, said Bonny, that you will read this semester are: The *Upanishads*, The *Bhagavad Gita*, The *Ramayana*, The *Mahabharata*, The *Kama Sutra*, The *Bible*, The *Tao Te Ching*, The Writings of Confucius, *The Emerald Tablet*, and The *Quran*. Feel free to read them in any order you choose, and don't hesitate to ask questions.

Welcome, said Pablo, to "Where-101."
Today's question is: "Where did farming begin?"

No, said Morton, I haven't seen any worms.

Sure, said Chelsea, I'd love to see your den.

Yes, said Glouster, the ducks are in very fine form.

All right, said Frank, who's hogging the *Kama Sutra*?

For Paul Cézanne, said Bonny, a landscape was a collection of geometrical shapes.

Excellent! said Bonny.

I like to watch the patterns, thought Ditto,
the insects make on the stream.

I like to watch the patterns, thought Blurtso,
the people make on the street.

Why do you think people do what they do?
I believe, said Pablo, that almost everything is a
desperate cry for attention. That's pathetic, said Blurtso.

Let's see, what shall I blog today?

Today's question, said Harlan, is: "Where did it go?"

Where did what go? said Chelsea.

It was here just a minute ago, said Morton.

It was? said Glouster.

I think so, said Morton.

I didn't take it, said Emma Lou.

Neither did I, said Frank.

Do you mean "ubi sunt"? said Glouster.

Ubi sunt? said Morton.

"Ubi sunt," said Glouster, is Latin for "Where are they?"
It comes from a Latin poem that begins, "Ubi sunt qui ante
nos in mundo fuere?" which translates: "Where are they
who, before us, existed in the world?" It was a common
theme in medieval poetry, and was most famously ex-
pressed by the French poet, François Villon who asked,

"Où sont les neiges d'antan?" or "Where are the snows of yesteryear?"

The snows of yesteryear? said Morton.

I don't like snow, said Chelsea.

Neither do I, said Frank.

I don't mind it, said Emma Lou, so long as I'm not far from my den.

Why would anyone worry about last year's snow? said Morton.

It's a metaphor, said Glouster, for all the things you've lost in your life.

Lost? said Chelsea.

Yes, said Glouster, the things you had in the past that you no longer have.

The things I've eaten? said Morton.

Yes, said Glouster, and the friends you've lost, and your lost youth.

My lost youth? said Chelsea.

Yes, said Glouster.

I'm not going to lose my youth, said Chelsea.

Of course you are, said Glouster.

Really? said Chelsea.

Yes, said Glouster.

In that case, said Chelsea, I don't like "ubi sunt."

Crows live forever, said Frank.

They do? said Morton.

Sure, said Frank, crows, or "ravens", and nightingales, and even some other birds.

Are you sure? said Morton.

Yes, said Frank, just ask Edgar Allen Poe and John Keats.

Who are *they*? said Chelsea.

They are poets, said Frank, who wrote about birds who live forever, birds who travel from heaven to earth to hell and then back again.

Have you been to heaven and hell? said Chelsea.

No, said Frank, not yet.

I don't want to go to hell, said Morton.

Heaven and hell, said Glouster, are metaphors for, "the realm of the dead."

I don't want to go there either, said Morton.

Maybe, said Chelsea, that's where the "ubi sunts" are.

I know a song, said Frank, about "ubi sunt."

What's it called? said Chelsea.

It's called "The Ash Grove," said Frank, and it has a blackbird in it.

How does it go? said Chelsea.

I don't remember all the words, said Frank, but it's about a woman who loses her lover and looks for him in an ash grove.

Does she find him? said Chelsea.

No, said Frank, he's buried beneath the green turf.

Is that a metaphor for "the realm of the dead"? said Morton.

Yes, said Frank.

Why doesn't the blackbird, said Chelsea, fly to the realm of the dead, talk to the dead lover, then return and talk to the woman so she can have a sense of closure?

That's a good question, said Frank.

What's closure? said Morton.

Closure, said Chelsea, is talking with your ex-lover until you have nothing more to say.

Why would you want to do that? said Morton.

Because, said Chelsea, if you say everything you have to say, you can stop thinking about him when he's gone.

So he doesn't become an "ubi sunt"? said Morton.

Yes, said Chelsea.

I would like to be an "ubi sunt", said Emma Lou.

So would I, said Glouster.

Why? said Chelsea.

Because, said Glouster, I don't want to be forgotten.

Being forgotten, said Emma Lou, would be like a second death.

Maybe it's a good thing, said Morton, for people to go around asking "ubi sunt?"

Why? said Chelsea.

Because, said Morton, it keeps the dead from dying.

Do you think the pumpkin pie is ready? said Morton.

I don't want to appear anxious, said Emma Lou.

Neither do I, said Chelsea.

How long should we wait? said Morton.

Until it's time, said Emma Lou.

How will we know? said Morton.

They'll tell us, said Emma Lou.

What if they don't? said Morton.

Then we'll never know, said Chelsea.

They'll tell us, said Emma Lou, if they want us to know.

And if they don't? said Morton.

Then they won't tell us, said Emma Lou.

That makes sense, said Chelsea.

Where are the others? said Morton.

They're waiting for us to decide, said Chelsea.

They don't want to appear anxious, said Emma Lou.

What's wrong with appearing anxious? said Morton.

It makes you look greedy, said Emma Lou.

Even if you're willing to share? said Morton.

Maybe they want us to wait, said Chelsea.

Why? said Morton.

Because anticipation increases desire, said Emma Lou.

Yes, said Chelsea, like in the *Kama Sutra*.

The *Kama Sutra*? said Morton.

The *Kama Sutra*, said Chelsea, is one of the books on our reading list.

The one the moose keeps hogging? said Morton.

Yes, said Chelsea, but I managed to sneak a peak.

What does it say? said Morton.

It says that withholding pleasure increases desire, and increasing desire increases pleasure.

What if you don't get what you desire? said Morton.

Then you still get the pleasure of anticipating, said Chelsea.

The pleasure of anticipating? said Morton.

Yes, said Chelsea, like when you spend the winter anticipating the spring fashions, and when the fashions come out, you're a little disappointed, but at least you had the pleasure of anticipating them.

That happens for me, said Emma Lou, every season of the year.

But sometimes when you get something, said Morton, it's as good as what you had hoped for.

That's true, said Chelsea, but getting it doesn't diminish the pleasure you got from anticipating it.

It teaches you, said Emma Lou, to enjoy the journey and not to focus on the destination.

The destination? said Morton.

The object of desire, said Emma Lou.

We've waited long enough, said Morton.

You may be right, said Emma Lou.

I wonder if Frank and Glouster are enjoying the wait? said Chelsea.

Birds can be very patient, said Emma Lou.

That's true, said Morton, I watched Frank sit on a fence for five hours yesterday.

You watched him for five hours? said Chelsea.

Yes, said Morton.

And you didn't get impatient? said Chelsea.

No, said Morton, I didn't want to eat him.

So you're only impatient, said Emma Lou, with things you want to consume?

Yes, said Morton.

What if you're not hungry? said Emma Lou.

There are some things I want to consume, said Morton, whether I'm hungry or not.

That's not very healthy, said Emma Lou.

I know, said Morton.

The question for today's class, said Blurtso, is: "What is the difference between sympathy and empathy?"

"Sympathy," said Glouster, is "a relationship between persons or things wherein whatever affects one similarly affects the other."

And empathy? said Chelsea.

"Empathy," said Glouster, is "the capacity for experiencing as one's own the feelings of another."

That sounds like the same thing, said Frank.

Both words, said Glouster, come from the Greek word, "pathos," meaning, "suffering, emotion, passion." In Greek "sym" means "with" and "em" means "in." So sympathy is suffering "with" another, while empathy is suffering "in" another.

Isn't that the same as compassion? said Emma Lou.

"Compassion," said Glouster, is "sorrow or pity aroused by the suffering of another." It is from the Latin words "com" meaning "with" and "passion" meaning "suffering."

So "compassion," said Emma Lou, is the Latin equivalent of the Greek word "sympathy."

Yes, said Glouster.

That still doesn't tell me, said Morton, the difference between sympathy and empathy.

Both words, said Glouster, imply a relationship or

"oneness" between the subject and object, between the "sympathizer" and the other.

The Upanishads, said Emma Lou, and the *Tao Te Ching* talk about the oneness of all things.

The gospel of Matthew, said Glouster, says "love your enemies," and the gospel of John says, "do unto others as you would have them do unto you."

Isn't that compassion? said Chelsea.

"Compassion," said Emma Lou, is feeling someone else's pain as your own. The way to do that is not to see others as separate from you.

One hundred fourteen of the one hundred fifteen verses of the *Quran*, said Frank, begin with "In the name of Allah the compassionate, the merciful..."

Ommmm, said moose.

What? said Glouster.

I think he said "Ommmm," said Frank.

Ommmm (phonetically "aum"), said Emma Lou, is from the Upanishads, it is the monosyllable which contains all syllables and all sounds. It represents the oneness underlying multiplicity—the non-duality of "Brahman" beneath the dualism and illusion of "Maya."

The illusion of Maya? said Morton.

The illusion that we are not all one, said Emma Lou.

I still don't understand, said Morton, the difference between sympathy and empathy.

Think of it this way, said Glouster. When someone is suffering because of a specific situation, but you have not experienced that situation yourself, you can only sympathize with them, but if you have experienced that same situation, you can empathize.

That's very confusing, said Chelsea.

Yes, said Morton, I feel exactly the same way.

Yes, said Bonny, snow is always white when it's new.

No, said Bonny, the river never flows back.

I can hear the last train, thought Pablo. The night animals will be out. Tomorrow I'll see their tracks in the snow. It must be exciting, moving quietly, feeling the pulse in your temples, seeing the hills in the grey light, and hearing the slender sound of the creek... maybe I should go for a walk.

Pablo? Please come to bed...

Look at the top of that tree, thought Ditto.
I wonder if it's windy up there, and frightening, and cold?
I wonder what it would be like to grow
so high up and exposed, day after day after day?

Aging, said Bonny, is the growth of deterioration.

Welcome, said Bonny.

What should we do? said Bonny. I don't know, said Pablo, what do you think, Blurtso? I don't know, what do you think, Bonny? I don't know, what do you think, Pablo?

Really? said Blurtso. We can skate with the ducks?

Doo dee doo dee doo, dee dee dee dee.

What a great day, said Blurtso. Yes, said Bonny, as good
as it gets. What shall we do now? I don't know, said
Pablo, how about a story? Yes, said Blurtso, a story! A story about a handsome and valorous donkey, or a sailor
who sails the seven seas in search of fortune and fame!

49

Well, said Pablo, I've been reading a novel titled, *The Adventures of Captain Harvey*, perhaps I could read a chapter out loud. What's it about? said Bonny. It's about a character, said Pablo, called Captain Harvey, who has the ability to take on the personality of whomever or whatever he encounters. Like a chameleon? said Blurtso. Yes, said Pablo. Is he a donkey? said Blurtso. No, said Pablo. Is he a sailor in search of fame and fortune? Yes, said Pablo, he is a sailor, but in this chapter he's not at sea, instead he's at a village in the mountains north of Rome, and has been taken in by a middle-aged couple, Elio and Agnese, and their adopted servant girl, Fiammetta. That sounds interesting, said Bonny. Yes, said Blurtso, please read the chapter! Alright, said Pablo, it begins like this...

"While the days were dedicated to caring for the animals, bringing wood and water, and preparing meals, the nights were passed in front of the fire, as the four residents and whatever neighbors happened to stop in would settle down to talk.

Early on, the conversation would focus on what work had been done that day, and what remained for tomorrow, and then it would turn to the latest report of rumors. At some point, Elio would excuse himself to join his friends at the bar. On this night, Agnese scolded him.

"Always the bar? Aren't *we* good company?"

"Good company?" said Elio. "Fiammetta says nothing, and you and Harvey go on like old women!"

"Well!" said Agnese. "If *you* ever said something... Why don't you tell a story? You used to tell such fine ones. I'm sure Harvey would enjoy one."

As Elio paused to consider which story he might tell, a stream of protagonists, antagonists, climaxes and anti-climaxes rushed through his head, but before he could choose one, Harvey began for him:

"Filomena was fifteen years old," said the captain, "when her grandmother told her, 'If you want your child to be a boy, you must sleep on your right side and have your midwife use water in which a murderer has washed his hands…'"

Elio was relieved, for he was too tired to make something up, and he liked having stories told him, because then it was real and not just remembering, so he put a log on the fire and sat back down in his place.

The story Harvey told, though taken directly from Elio's memory, was not as Elio remembered it, for just as the log began to crackle and whine in the fire, it altered the captain's tale until the listeners could hear the cracking of a whip, or the cries of a forsaken child, or the moans of an impassioned lover. What our hero told, in fact, was the history of the life of the log, of its stored energies released into the arms of the air. The listeners were enthralled. Even the romantic encounters, which surprised them with their attention to detail, were done with such delicacy that Agnese could not be offended, and Fiammetta moved into the light.

As the days passed Harvey became quite popular in the town; everyone liked his receptive nature and his knowledge of Abruzzese traditions, and he was often invited to drink in the bar, or skate with the children on the pond, or play in the tournaments of two-king chess. Elio was the undisputed champion and he found in Captain Harvey his first worthy opponent.

They would play chess until evening when the guests arrived, and Elio would get up to stoke the fire while Harvey prepared the night's story. The group would listen, apprehensively at first, wondering if he would improvise or tell a stock tale from one of their memories. If it was early, he would spin the yarn leisurely, amplifying here and interpolating there, always going on in a steady, gentle voice, except when he impersonated a man or woman in the throes of passion or a demon in a fit of rage. Then he would pause, anticipating with his silence the pleasure certain to come, and as the fire began to wane the pauses would become shorter and less frequent, and he would bring the story to an end, reuniting lost lovers or reconciling the hero to his fate, and leaving the group with a feeling at once of fulfillment and loss.

Each story was different, taking its theme from the nature of the wood. There were stories of those who reached the happy end they had sought, or those who obtained what they desired or regained what they had lost, or those for whom love had an unhappy ending, or those who won happiness after grief and misfortune, and each tale was born of the same fiery source. It was not long before Harvey began to look at everyone he met in terms of the fire. What kind of flame was Elio? Was his wood slow and deep, or superficial and smoldering at the edges? What was Agnese? What was Fiammetta? What was he…?

It's not snowing anymore, said Bonny.
Shall we walk Blurtso to the station?

What should we do now? said Pablo.
Let's go home, said Bonny, and play Sudoku.

Let's see... that's 127 for Ditto,
96 for me, and 12 for Pablo.

Why is that tree different? said Bonny. Because it's dying.
Why is it dying? Because it's old. Its roots can't nourish it,
and its leaves don't absorb the sun. Save it? No, we can't
save it. It's going to die, and then it will fall, and rot, and
become food for the forest. You and me? Yes, one day.

I'm worried about Ditto, said Bonny. Why? said Pablo.
Because he's spending too much time with that tree.

Go fish, said Ditto.

A eulogy? said Bonny. Yes, I could say something... "Here lies a tree. It was a good tree. A tree that made use of what was offered, and offered what made use. It grew without haste, and it grew without malice. And when it fell, it made a sound."

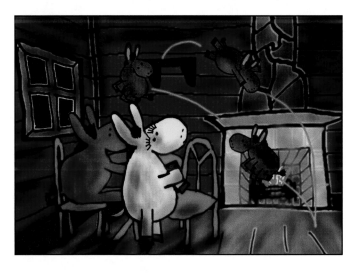

Maybe it's time to put Ditto in school...

What, said the schoolmarm, do *you* want?

O.k., said the schoolmarm, who would like to try
the next equation? How about you in the second row,
the one with the boxing-glove nose...

I don't think Ditto liked his first day of school...

Hello, said Virginia, my name is Virginia.
Hello, said Ditto. Would you like a hay sandwich?

Ditto's walking home alone for the first time.
He'll be fine, said Pablo, do we have any more wine?

It's time to practice reading, said the schoolmarm.
Virginia, will you begin on page one?
"Here is Spot," read Virginia, "See Spot run. See Spot play."
Excellent! said the schoolmarm.

O.k. "big-nose," please continue from page two hundred thirty two. "Twas brillig," read Ditto, "and the slithy toves did gyre and gimble in the wabe; all mimsy were the borogoves, and the mome raths outgrabe... he went galumphing back... hast thou slain the Jabberwock?"

Virginia, said the schoolmarm, would you please do the first equation? How much is three plus three?
Three plus three, said Virginia, is six.
Excellent! said the schoolmarm.

O.k., said the schoolmarm, let's have "big-nose" do the next one... Tell us, big-nose, how many arc seconds per century is the perihelion precession of Mercury relative to the earth, and what scientist provided the theory to explain this precession?

Your assignment is to draw an apple...

Excellent, Virginia!

No, no, no big-nose! I said an apple! Just an apple!

Your assignment is to draw a house...

Excellent, Virginia!

No, no, no big-nose! I said a house! Just a house!

It's a blustery, snow-swept day at Fenway…
here's the pitch… Jeter hits a scorcher to second…
Dustin "Ditto" Pedroia glides over… scoops… throws...

Spring is here, said Virginia, only two more months before summer vacation. Summer vacation? said Ditto. Yes, said Virginia. What's summer vacation? said Ditto. That's when we get three months off before coming back to school. Coming back? said Ditto. Yes, said Virginia, in the fall. For how long? said Ditto. Until the next summer, said Virginia. And then? said Ditto. Until the summer after that, said Virginia. How long do we have to keep coming? Forever, said Virginia. Forever? said Ditto. Yes, said Virginia, until we grow old.

The Benchmark test is on Friday. Benchmark? said Ditto. Yes, said Virginia, the test that decides if we will be a failure or a success. A failure, said Ditto, in first grade? Yes, said Virginia, if you fail they put you in a special class with all the other failures. That's not fair, said Ditto, I'm too young to die.

"Blah, blah, blah," said the schoolmarm, "blah, blah, blah, blah." This lesson is so boring, thought Ditto. I think my hind legs have fallen asleep. Yes, my left hind leg is asleep, and my right leg is tingling. I wonder why that happens? Maybe my nerves are impinged by the way I'm sitting, or my arteries are squeezed. I wonder how much I'd have to move to make my leg come back? I wonder if wiggling my ears would make a difference? Or twitching my nose? Maybe if I flexed the muscles in my thigh… yes, that works… my left leg is coming back … and my right leg isn't tingling… but my tail has gone numb… I wonder why that happens? Maybe they will kick me out of school if I fail the Bench-mark… I wonder how bad you have to be to get kicked out? I can be pretty bad if I try. Yes, I'm sure I'm smart enough to get kicked out of school… I mean, really… how hard can it be?

Nonsense Word Fluency

boc	kib	ul	jan	lel
fic	kum	jax	oj	dev
waz	pej	yos	mun	fiv
ec	faj	vog	kil	pux

"boc?" said Ditto, What's a "boc?" Just read the word, said the schoolmarm. But "boc" isn't a word, said Ditto. Just read the word, said the schoolmarm. But it doesn't make sense, said Ditto. Just read the word, said the schoolmarm. But there aren't any words, said Ditto. Just read the word, said the schoolmarm. This isn't English, said Ditto. Just read the word, said the schoolmarm. Can I use a Rosetta stone? said Ditto, or the Pentagon's decoding program? Just read the word, said the schoolmarm. Or maybe a soothsayer? said Ditto. Just read the word, said the schoolmarm. Or a deck of Tarot cards? said Ditto. Stop! said the schoolmarm. Your time's up! You scored one out of forty, you're a red light. A red light? said Ditto. Yes, said the schoolmarm, an abject failure, you'll start intervention in the morning.

An abject failure? said Virginia. Yes, said Ditto, that's what the teacher called me. I've never heard the word "abject," said Virginia. "Abject," said Ditto, refers to someone cast down in spirit, someone reduced to hopelessness or despair. Really? said Virginia. Yes, said Ditto, at least that's the way Thoreau uses it. Thoreau? said Virginia. Henry David Thoreau, said Ditto, a man who wrote a book called *Walden*—my parents have a copy and they let me read it. Was Thoreau abject? said Virginia. No, said Ditto, just the opposite. How come you can read *Walden*, said Virginia, but can't pass the Benchmark? I don't know, said Ditto, I guess Thoreau's kind of writing has been outlawed.

Intervention? said Virginia. Yes, said Ditto, every day during lunch I have to meet with a special teacher. Until when? said Virginia. Until I pass the next Benchmark. What if you fail the next one? Then I continue to be intervened.

Hello, said Ms. Johnson, I'm Ms. Johnson. Hello, said Ditto, I'm Ditto. Nice to meet you, Ditto. Nice to meet you, Ms. Johnson. I understand, said Ms. Johnson, that you had

some trouble with the Benchmark test. Yes, said Ditto, the words didn't make any sense. Didn't the teacher explain, said Ms. Johnson, that the words were make-believe words? Yes, said Ditto, but even make-believe words have meaning. I don't understand, said Ms. Johnson. Aren't all words, said Ditto, make-believe words? All words? said Ms. Johnson. Yes, said Ditto, the word "tree" has no ontological relationship to the thing we call a tree. We might invent any word and make believe it refers to a tree. In fact, the word for tree is different in every language that exists, and all the different words are simply make-believe words that we've agreed upon to refer to trees.

You're exactly right, said Ms. Johnson. And if someone is asked to read a group of make-believe words, said Ditto, how do they know that the words don't have make-believe pronunciations? They don't know, said Ms. Johnson, be-cause the group of make-believe words might constitute a make-believe language, with its own grammar, syntax, and pronunciation. Exactly, said Ditto, that's why I had trouble with the test. Would it have helped, said Ms. Johnson, if the schoolmarm had said the words were "meaningless"? Meaningless? said Ditto. How could they be called meaningless if they've determined where I have to spend my lunch hour? Yes, said Ms. Johnson, the two of us are going to get along very, very well.

 I spoke to the schoolmarm, said Ms. Johnson, about your difficulty with the Benchmark. What did she say? said Ditto. She said that it doesn't matter why you failed the test, you'll have to remain in intervention until the next test at the end of May. That's fine with me, said Ditto. Good, said Ms. Johnson, I thought we might do a "read aloud." I brought a book called, *The Children's Story*, by a writer named James Clavell. James Clavell? said Ditto, the author of *Shogun*? Yes, said Ms. Johnson, have you seen the movie? No, said Ditto, but I read the novel.

I like your house, said Virginia. Thank you, said Ditto. How is the intervention class? I love it, said Ditto, we're reading a book by James Clavell. James Clavell? said Virginia. Yes, said Ditto, and Ms. Johnson asks all kinds of interest-  ing questions, and she lets me answer any way I choose. Really? said Virginia. Really, said Ditto. It's not like our regular class? said Virginia. No, said Ditto, we talk about whatever the story brings to mind. That's great, said Virginia. Yes it is, said Ditto, you should try to get in. To intervention? said Virginia. Yes, said Ditto. How? said

Virginia. What was your Benchmark score? said Ditto. I was a yellow light, said Virginia. Maybe if you failed your weekly tests, said Ditto, you could become a red light. Do you think? said Virginia. I don't know, said Ditto, it's worth a try.

Hello, said Ms. Johnson, my name is Ms. Johnson. Hello, said Virginia, my name is Virginia. Now that Virginia is with us, said Ms. Johnson, we'll go back to the beginning and start our book again. Is that o.k., Ditto? Of course, said Ditto, I loved the beginning. Very well, said Ms. Johnson, the first page of *The Children's Story* says:

The teacher was afraid. And the children were afraid. All except Johnny. He watched the classroom door with hate. He felt the hatred deep within his stomach. It gave him strength. It was two minutes to nine.

That's a strange beginning, said Virginia, it doesn't even say "once upon a time." No, it doesn't, said Ms. Johnson. Why not? said Virginia. Because the story, said Ms. Johnson, doesn't begin at the beginning. Why not? said Virginia. That's a good question, said Ms. Johnson, what do you think? I don't know, said Virginia. I think, said Ditto, that the author doesn't want us to know the beginning. Why not? Because, said Ditto, if he doesn't tell us the beginning we have to guess, and to guess we have to pay attention to the middle. Very good! said Ms. Johnson.

Like a riddle? said Virginia. Yes, said Ms. Johnson. Or a game of twenty questions? said Virginia. Yes, said Ms. Johnson, except that we're never sure of the answer. Why not? said Virginia. Because, said Ms. Johnson, the author never tells us the beginning, even when the story is over. So how can we be sure of anything? said Virginia. We can't, said Ms. Johnson. I don't like that, said Virginia. Why not? said Ms. Johnson. Because, said Virginia, I like to be sure.

Why do you like to be sure? said Ms. Johnson. Because, said Virginia, if I'm sure of something I can tell if it's right or wrong. How much information do you need, said Ms. Johnson, to be sure? All of it, said Virginia. All of it? said Ms. Johnson, is that possible? No, said Ditto, it's impossible to know everything. So how can we be sure? said Ms. Johnson. We can't, said Ditto, not completely. But we make judgments every day, said Ms. Johnson, and act on those judgments. Yes, said Ditto, but we can't be sure those judgments are right. But lots of people, said Virginia, are sure they're right. Yes they are, said Ms. Johnson. Maybe, said Ditto, they should read this book. Yes, said Ms. Johnson, maybe they should.

 I don't like Johnny, said Virginia. Why not? said Ms. Johnson. Because, said Virginia, he's filled with hate. Is hate a bad thing? said Ms. Johnson. Yes, said Virginia, very bad. But his hatred, said Ms. Johnson, makes him strong... is strength a bad thing? No, said Virginia, it's a good thing. So a bad thing, said Ms. Johnson, can create a good thing? That doesn't make sense, said Virginia. Maybe, said Ditto, there is good in bad things, and bad in good things. That makes even less sense, said Virginia. Why? said Ms. Johnson. Because bad is bad, said Virginia, and good is good.

Is a tiger bad? said Ms. Johnson. No, said Virginia, I love tigers! What if one of those tigers ate Ditto? That would be a bad tiger! said Virginia. But it's the same tiger, said Ms. Johnson. Yes, said Virginia. So good things can become bad, said Ms. Johnson, in certain situations? And bad things can become good, said Ditto, like Johnny's hatred.

Hmm, said Virginia, how come we never have discussions like this in our regular class? Because, said Ms. Johnson, your regular class is scripted. Scripted? said Virginia. Yes, said Ms. Johnson, what the schoolmarm says is prepared by the Department of Education, and she reads the script they tell her to read. Why don't they give her a good script? said Virginia. Because they think it *is* a good script. But it isn't, said Virginia, it's a bad script. I think it's a good script, said Ditto. Why? said Ms. Johnson. Because, said Ditto, if it weren't such a bad script, I wouldn't have failed my test and been put in this class, and this is a very good class with a very good script.

I'm going to say two words, said the schoolmarm, tell me which begins with "eh." Listen carefully: egg, pan. Which word begins with "eh"? Egg begins with "eh." Now, I'm going to say two more words. Tell me which begins with "h"... I wonder, thought Virginia, what Ditto is thinking? It looks like he's paying attention. I never realized how boring this class was until I got put in intervention. We never say what we think. We just repeat. I wonder if the schoolmarm likes what she does? I guess grown-ups don't get bored as easy as kids.

Do you think we're dumb? said Virginia. Dumb? said
Ditto. Yes, said Virginia, because we're in the class for
failures. But you failed on purpose, said Ditto. Yes, said
Virginia, but maybe I'm too dumb to find the regular class
interesting. I'm not dumb, said Ditto, and I don't find the
regular class interesting. Then why did you fail the Benchmark? My mother, said Ditto, says I failed because donkeys
have a different way of understanding. A different way?
said Virginia. Yes, said Ditto, we're donkeycentric. Donkeycentric? said Virginia. Yes, said Ditto, we understand
things based on our experience as donkeys.

Is Ms. Johnson donkeycentric? said Virginia. Partly, said
Ditto, she's multicentric. Multicentric? said Virginia. Yes,
said Ditto, she understands things from multiple perspec-
tives. How can she do that? said Virginia. She's not bound
by any limits, said Ditto, and her center is everywhere.

"Blah, blah, blah," said the school-marm, "blah, blah, blah, blah." This lesson is so boring, thought Ditto. I wonder how the school-marm gets her hair like that? It's almost like a block of clay... or a wasps' nest... or a bunch of cow-pies stacked on top of each other and glued with construction paste... I like the smell of construction paste... but I don't like the taste... I prefer the taste of alfalfa... that's an interesting word... alfalfa.. three a's... two l's... and two f's... hmm... it's almost a palindrome... aflafla... I wonder if it tastes just as good when it's spelled backwards... or when you eat it upside down...

Ditto and Virginia, said Pablo, are enjoying their new class. Yes, said Bonny, it's good for them to be exposed to the process of Socratic dialectic, and to the limitation of words.

What? said Virginia. Did you say something?
No, said Ditto, I didn't say anything.

"Blah, blah, blah," said the schoolmarm, "blah, blah, blah, blah." This lesson is so boring, thought Ditto. I wonder what the schoolmarm is saying? It's hard to focus with that little piece of corn between her teeth. I wonder if she knows it's there? I wonder what else she had for lunch? There's a spot on the sleeve of her blouse… maybe she had a Salisbury steak with gravy… or a donut with chocolate icing… or maybe it's blood… maybe she smashed a mosquito with her elbow… or leaned against a freshly painted barn… the spot matches the color of her shoes… I wonder if she ties her laces with a single loop or bunny ears through the rabbit hole… one of the laces is loose… and an ear has come undone… I haven't seen many bunnies this spring… maybe I'll see one on the way home… if I'm lucky… maybe I'll see a bunny… or a turtle… or a giraffe…

Have you noticed, said Ditto, that the schoolmarm doesn't call on me as much? Maybe, said Virginia, she's given up on you. Yes, said Ditto, I sure hope so.

Some artists, said Bonny, believe that perspective determines reality, and painters should paint things from many points of view.

Excellent! said Bonny.

The art of painting, said Bonny, is to capture
one of life's moments on canvas.
The art of life is to let those moments go.

Excellent! said Bonny.

 "Blah, blah, blah," said the school-marm, "blah, blah, blah, blah." Tomorrow is the last day of school, thought Ditto. I can't believe it's almost over. I would never have survived without Ms. Johnson. I wish Ms. Johnson was the regular teacher. I wonder if we could go on strike? If the people in a republic can choose their leader, why can't the children in a school choose their teacher? We wouldn't have to cut up the flag, or do all the tricky things the New Teacher does in *The Children's Story*. I wonder if I could convince my classmates? Most of them seem content with the schoolmarm, repeating what she says. But they've never met Ms. Johnson. It's hard to get people to like someone they've never met… or get people to change at all… but I'll bet I could change them… yes, it might be tricky, but I'll bet I could…

What are you going to do for the summer?
I don't know, said Ditto. What are you going to do?
I don't know, said Virginia.

The semester is over? said Morton.

Yes, said Harlan.

What should we do now?

Whatever you want, said Harlan.

What are *you* going to do? said Morton.

Me? said Chelsea. I've got a million things to do.

What about you, Frank?

I'm going to visit my friends in Concord.

Concord? said Morton.

Yes, said Frank, the Sleepy Hollow Cemetery.

How about you, Glouster?

I'm going to spend the summer with my family under the Longfellow Bridge.

And you, Emma Lou?

I'm going to remodel my burrow.

Oh, said Morton.

Hello, said Pablo. Hello, said Morton. What are you doing at Walden Pond? I don't know, said Morton. You don't know? said Pablo. No, said Morton. Be careful you don't get bitten by any deer ticks. Deer ticks? said Morton. Yes, said Pablo, spring is the season for deer ticks. Oh, said Morton. Where are the other students? said Pablo. Glouster is in Boston with his family at Longfellow bridge, Chelsea is shopping, Emma Lou is remodeling her burrow, Frank is visiting the Concord cemetery, and the moose just vanished. Do you have any plans for the summer? No, said Morton, I can't figure out what to do. Maybe you should spend the summer here. Here? said Morton. Sure, said Pablo. What could I do here? said Morton. You could look at things, said Pablo, and listen to things, and write about what you see and hear. Really? said Morton. Sure, said Pablo, just like Thoreau. Who? said Morton. Henry David Thoreau, said Pablo, a man who didn't know what to do after he graduated from college, and moved to Walden to write about what he saw and heard. That doesn't sound very interesting, said Morton. Actually, said Pablo, he became famous. Really? said Morton, just because he didn't know what to do after college?

"Sights" – Many trees. A lot of last year's leaves. And oh yes, I saw a bug that might have been a deer tick. But since I've never seen a deer tick, I can't be sure. I suppose you can't be sure about something until you can.

"Sights" – Lots of trees. More trees. Sunlight through the trees. Shadows of the trees. Sometimes the shadows are blown around by the wind, but are never completely blown away.

"Sounds" – Birds. The wind. The sloshing of the pond against the shore. And the sound of an airplane. I think it was from an airplane. Because I didn't hear the sound when I first saw the plane, then I heard the sound and saw the plane, then I didn't see the plane but I still heard the sound. Maybe the wind blows sound like it blows shadows.

What do you think crows talk about? said Virginia. I don't know, said Ditto, probably what everyone else does.

Really? said Frank. A worm-finding app on your iPhone?

Is that your iPhone ringing? said Ditto.
No, said Virginia, I don't have an iPhone.

Nevermore? said Frank. Isn't that a bit pessimistic?

"Sounds" – Birds. More birds. And the sound of the wind. I don't know how something you can't see can make so much noise.

"Tastes" - Grass. Flowers. Oh, and I think I accidentally ate a deer tick. But since I don't know what a deer tick tastes like, I can't be sure. I suppose you can't be sure of what you're eating until you can.

"Tastes" – The grass that grows around last year's leaves. The flowers. Today I ate a white flower that tasted like the yellow one I ate yesterday. Sometimes different flowers taste the same and sometimes they don't. Sight and taste are not always connected.

"Sights" - Clouds. Lots of clouds. Then one big cloud. A cloud that covered the whole lake and maybe even the world. Everything was whitish grey. It erased the shadows of the leaves and trees. I suppose it sucked them into itself which is why the cloud was dark in spots. It also sucked up sounds. The train wasn't as noisy, and the birds sang a lower pitch.

"Sights" - More clouds. Cloud. Covering the lake...
stealing the blue from the water.

"Sounds": Rainfall. Cloudburst. I suppose the cloud got so full with all the things it sucked up, it had to spit them out—the sounds, the colors, the smells. The raindrops gathered together when they hit the ground and began to run around making noises and spreading flashes of color. They ran down my nose and flanks and haunches and tail, and found the holes in my shelter I could only hear before. Rain makes it easy to see holes, and it makes silent things reveal their sound. Like the stone outside my shelter that never made a sound until the rain came and all the nooks and crannies sang.

"Sights": Sunshine through the clouds. Silver drops on the leaves and ground. Mud and bits of leaves on my hooves and ankles. Patches of blue spilled on the lake.

"Smells" - Rain on the wind. Another storm approaching. And something I don't recognize. Possibly the smell of a deer tick. But I've never smelled a deer tick before, so I can't be sure. I suppose you can't be sure of what you're smelling until you are.

"Sights": My home in ruins. Blown to the ground by last night's storm. No more cracks where the wind made noise. No more shade. No shelter. Just a heap of boards. And the wet ground.

"Sounds" – My breath. Panting as I propped up the walls of my shelter. I didn't even hear the train to Concord because I was so focused on building. You can only hear what you happen to be listening to, or else the sound of building ate up the sound of the train.

"Tastes" - Thinking about eating. Me eating grass. Clouds eating colors. Sounds eating sounds and ticks eating me... even thoughts eating thoughts. Everything a big circle of eating.

"Sounds" – The echo of an axe. Pablo. I helped him stack wood in the shed behind his cabin. He said I should gather some.

94

"Sounds" – Another day with Pablo. Listening to him talk to me and listening to me talk to him. I could also hear Bonny and Ditto by the lake, I think they were painting because I could smell the paint. There were large patches of silence between the words they were saying. Or maybe the patches of silence were when I was listening to Pablo or myself talk.

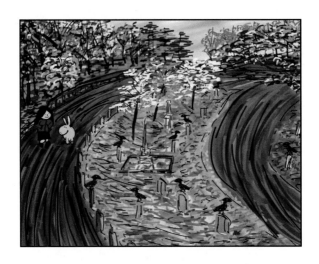

Crows are messengers of the dead? Yes, said Virginia, that's what my uncle said. Dead humans or dead donkeys? Dead humans, said Virginia. Hmm, said Ditto, I wonder which animals are messengers of dead crows?

What is it? said Virginia. It's a pencil. A pencil? Yes, said Ditto. Who does it belong to? I don't know. Maybe we should take it to town, said Virginia, and ask around.

Well, said Virginia, no one in Concord is missing a pencil.
No, said Ditto, they looked at us like we were crazy. I
guess people don't use pencils anymore, said Virginia.
No, said Ditto, I guess not. What'll we do with it? If we
save it, said Ditto, it might become an antique. An antique? said Virginia. Yes, said Ditto, like putt putt boats,
cassette tapes, and common courtesy. And people would
travel for miles to see it? said Virginia. Yes, said Ditto,
and we'd keep it behind glass, and rent headphones to
explain its history. So the tourists would know what to
think? said Virginia. Yes, said Ditto, and realize how
important it is, and not complain about the admission fee.
And visitors would come to Concord from all over the
world! said Virginia. Yes, said Ditto.

"Smells" – Bonny and Pablo made a pumpkin pie. I could smell it from the other side of the lake. I walked to their cabin to tell them I could smell the pie, and they offered me a slice.

"Tastes" – The grass didn't taste as sweet this morning. I think it is because of last night's pie. I suppose flavors eat each other like one sound eats another. I wonder if a donkey doesn't taste as good to a deer tick after a deer tick has tasted a deer?

"Sounds" – I talked to Pablo about deer ticks and he told me their full name is "ixodes scapularis" and that they drink an animal's blood four to five days before letting go. He said they can spread lyme disease, but that humans are more susceptible than donkeys. Maybe that's why there aren't as many humans in the woods. Maybe now that I know more about deer ticks, they will be less interested in biting me.

"Thoughts" – I don't think I was bitten by a deer tick today.
Maybe knowledge is power.

"Thoughts" – Thoreau was wise to spend time in these
woods, there is so much to learn here. I guess a lot of people say they would like to live in the woods, but almost
none of them do it. Maybe that's one reason Thoreau
became famous—because what he wrote enables people
who live in big houses to read about living in a cabin. They
can experience it without really doing it. Maybe that's what
humans are looking for in life, to experience things without
really doing them. That would explain all the televisions
and computers and iPhones.

"Sights" – Fly in web. Struggling. Spider waiting.

"Sights" – Stillness of sky. Stillness of lake. Together in reflection. Clouds blown together, clouds blown apart. Spider, fly, eater and eaten, diner and dinner, survivor and snack... together in reflection.

. . . .

The less I am me, the more I am what I see and hear.
Perhaps the moment I become nothing,
I will become everything.

Where's your pencil? said Virginia. I left it at home, said Ditto. What about the tourists, said Virginia, and the audio phones? I'm not going to do it, said Ditto. Why? said Virginia. I like Concord the way it is. Yes, said Virginia, the Sleepy Hollow Cemetery, the Concord Museum, the Colonial Inn, and the friendly people at the Main Street Café—it's a lovely town, and more traffic might spoil it. Yes, said Ditto, and someone might even try to put a stop light on Main Street.